T0380229

# The

# COMPLEXITIES

## Of

# Nike & Athena

---

*Marcia Battise a Biography*

---

M A R C I A   B A T T I S E

Balboa Press books may be ordered through booksellers or by contacting:

Balboa Press
A Division of Hay House
1663 Liberty Drive
Bloomington, IN 47403
www.balboapress.com
1 (877) 407-4847

ISBN: 978-1-9822-4378-4 (sc)
ISBN: 978-1-9822-4379-1 (e)

Library of Congress Control Number: 2020915124

Print information available on the last page.

Balboa Press rev. date: 09/23/2020

**BALBOA**.PRESS
A DIVISION OF HAY HOUSE

**2019 WORLD CATASTROPHE AND GOING INTO
SOCIAL DISTANCING :**

<u>**Film Ref : TERMINATOR**</u>

**"DO You Remember Terminator?**
**Last scene of one of the film's where Sarah Connor's son and a General's daughter was trapped or barracaded in an army bunker/base – hiding form the terminators of that film, not knowing who was anywhere outside of their walls and what life was like, living in fear …. Thinking "We May Have To Start The Human Race Over Again!"**

**SOCIAL DISTANCING is phase two of COVID-19 CORONAVIRUS 2020**

<u>**THE GENERATION WHICH LET IT HAPPEN AGAIN**</u>

*Quote of the centur*
*"Free medicine, pls, no more than 2 – 4 at a time and 6ft apart standard"*

This generation has caused stresses beyond belief that even those of belief are turning to ALL conspiracy theories as to why these idiots who go via many names, have statues, awarded all sorts of prizes are unable to do what societies around the world have been asking them to do which is :

> *"PARTAKE IN THE MAKING OF THE CAKE*
> *SHARE IN THE EATING OF THE CAKE*
> *CLEAN UP AFTER BOTH*
> *REPLENISH FOR THE NEXT EATING OF THE CAKE".*

This has been a very underlined then forced issue of "what is wrong with a generation when the Generation has become unable to do the following –

Deal with the common cold.

Carry some weight, most of them will and do think that carrying weight is something you are paid for in job form, and in Job form the weight of carrying something has fell from 59lbs to 35/30lbs.

Participate with a positive idea to help humanities basic human grow and function as everyone has to carry some weight.

> *"GOD DAMN THE IDIOT WHO GOD HELPED WHO CAME FROM POOR*
> *BACKGROUNDS, NEEDED HELP, AND WAS SENT HELP THROUGH*
> *THE LOVING GUIDENCE OF GOD IN THE BASIC FORM OF :*
> *ANGELS, SPIRITS, HIGHER SELVES AND NATURE …..TO HELP THEIR MINDS*
> *FLOW AND BE NOURISHED WITH CREATIVITY TO DO THE CAKE".*

THE WORLD has gone into a MENTLE ressession as financially it has been shown to them through the eyes of the finance world, which many knew was in a WORLD RESSESSION and as a direct "GOD-SEND MESSAGE", that this is the time to do your own work personally and leave other people alone UNTIL your personal work with god has been done THROUGH THE USE OF YOUR HIGHER SELF.

## PROBLEM :

**SOCIAL DISTANCING IN THE WAKE OF COVID-19 CORONAVIRUS**

At present most people have died from this airbourne virus like a plague, last known was AIDS, most of the world has gone into quarantine, most of the world gone into lockdown which started before Easter 2020 – March, and most of the world is still thinking of extending while other countries state new aspects of the virus emerging as new cases of infection to deaths.

2020 in the charts of the spiritual initiates and masters IS A MASTER YEAR and we see the new introduction of metaphysics through a master like St Germain – THIS IS THE YEAR OF THE MENTAL and every being in earth is encouraged to find their way back to god as even nature has this problem when we look at how I'll our trees has become and how less their existence is then so on through nature to human.

If we cannot find our way back to the creator through the direct avenues given to us via the creator, if not for ourselves and not for the earth, then Moses and his tablet of instructions from the hills of communication become and mean nothing, Dr Fatus and his 7 sins mean nothing when he was told by god, DON'T DO THAT and so on.

**THE IGNORANCE of SOCIAL DISTANCING – This generations new selfies**

# "WHAT A GOD SEND!"

How do I justify this phrase during this period, how often have we jumped to this phrase?

*SOCIAL DISTANCING has in many opinions FRIGHTENED PEOPLE. The basic meaning and aspects of social DISTANCING is : PHYSICAL DISTANCING & REDUCE PRODUCTION.*

From since the early 5ᵗʰ century BCE and maybe before but around this time we have known this aspect of bullying via mind control to be effective and has been used in many ways to be "OF THE BENEFIT" of the people yet dished out as a benefit of those who know they do and are wrong or even mis-interpretatons of an event needed to show there is something wrong and to look for the causes of this wrongness. The last one I knew of was the 80s AIDS epidemic and that I experienced through all aspects of media just as we are doing the same with COVID-19 CORONAVIRUS.

THE aids period people made quilts which was how they used their creativity and that was my indigo generation, what are this generation doing who wear these millennial crowns, the indigo -gen x generation was and is to a degree a hated and misplaced generation of lack of understanding even into adulthood.

This generation has been told that they are focusing took much on the NON-PARTICIPAATION OF LIFE, over the last 5yrs or so, they have been warned to participate, as there is too much infighting amongst themselves and they are a huge generation of people within the population as a whole.

## HOW DO YOU BLAME A VIRUS LIKE COVID-19 CORONAVIRUS ON THEM?

Let's start with what I am doing right now;

**FOOD – THIS BOOK IS SOUL FOOD**
**MIND – THIS BOOK IS TO HELP MINDS**
**NUTRITION – THIS BOOK IS TO MAKE THEM AWARE OF THEIR HOME etc**

The avenues open to them is as we know via our basic 5 senses and the visual aspect is more prominent and dominate so moving images is the best and yet the most abused and that is entertainment in full on film of which they themselves have been eager to use in the aspect of sharing. The indigo were blamed for all the financial destruction. Examples are wall st which made society realise they meant it and woke up to people who were doing God's work since they felt like some were creating wars with god – In METAPHYSICS alone there are many ways this can be played out like a video game of war and the millennials seem to be playing it very well.

COVID-19 THE CORONAVIRUS is something that has been utilized to explore the question "How healthy is the human mind who does not listen, feel and participate?"

We have various aspects of free medicine through meditations which we are encouraged to do and these are with GUIDENCE from angels like Michael, Metratron and then their direct channels messages who tell the listeners that this is REALLY GODS message and there are those with masters like St GERMAINE who provide medicine in the form of the Violet Flame, and there are NATURES sounded meditations – these are all aspects of messages through music, voice and visuals and they state they are not imposters of God and to learn to trust your minded connection with god via these FREE MEDICINAL PRACTICES FOR THE MIND AS A WHOLE.

There is a saying or quote that God said do not create temple etc in the image of … The story of CIVID-19 CORONAVIRUS 2020 in a quick few lines as this has transformed through the theories of CON-SPI-RA-CY :

**WUHAN – CHINA**
**HUBEI – MARKET FOOD VILLAGE**
**HUANAN – NAME OF SEAFOOD MARKET**

Then the story developed into bats, pigs interacting with humans transferring this virus of corona into COVID-19 CORONAVIRUS. There are still many papers of examination been developed from the original location and determination of this food contamination which explained why the worlds food industry was hit with immediate and effective shutdown of ALL food places around the world, even though the out break spread into DIFFERENT aspects of human life the food industry including the drinking establishments were among the first at mass to be shut down and required to go into quarantine services – this meant cleaning aka DOMESTOS & CLOROX, these household products are known to fight, stop these airbourne virus and state that on the product, others like Dettol, zalflora & pine are other disinfectants used by households so on an economy platform through BUISNESS imagine what Starbucks, nandos, chipotle, MacDonald and then those recommended in your world travel Zagat guide has as cleaning sanitation products?

Then there's the world joke about toilets which we saw in most western countries that public toilets were becoming less and the sewage system was going through major upgrades due to some of been 50 years old and suffering from heavy corrosion, the LOS ANGELES CITY SEWER PROJECT is one example.

That is a a possibility that this thing could be seasonal as there STRING request for vaccinations which won't come out until about 2021 and you just need to seek out any reliable news channel, for me it's msnbc to hear about this and the testing kits like the standard drug testing kits which is scaring A LOT of people as this market is not fully regulated and even the president was accused of promoting, suggesting the use of something that was not officially tested or released by the health bodies who do these and state it is safe to use and will take responsibility for if systems arise from them. We are currently looking at two countries India and China who are fast in development making something WETHER it be temporary or a permanent fix for a vaccine to kill off this aspect of coronavirus as scientist have been saying it is a virus we know and are accustomed to!?!

HYGIENE – LOS ANGELES LIKE MANY MELTING POT CITIES AND OVER POPULATED CITIES IS DIRTY and been listed as one of the hardest hit within its home of California like NEW YORK STATE, for years the millennials have been asked about economical and greener ways to dispose of waste since they like to play with ARTIFICIAL INTELLIGENCE within societies technology and have seemed dispondent just like those who shied away from any factual evidence to global warming and the enhancements needed to make global warming UN-MYTHICAL.

Meaning, there is no logic to them if "It rains, water is on the ground, the sun shines, the water disappears".

That factual activity of the elements is called changes of climate which is marketed as CLIMATE CHANGE.

Now, where has the water gone?

I will leave you the readers, them the millennials and the academics and those of the AI world to investigate the above complicated system of changes of climate to figure out how in CLIMATE CHANGE aka GLOBAL WARMING, the economics with the help of TONY ROBBINS as he is a spiritual man of economics, to solve the above.

Going back to the MENTLE and THE MIND, in times of distress A LOT of people pull out variations of the bible (Donald Trump has), A Bible, A Book From God, A Spirit Book, A Meditation Mantra etc, we are at that stage where "SOCIAL MEDIA" HAS become one of the most important aspects of taking care of ourselves and there are books on this, especially in times of distress, the heart of people seems to be missing, many people live in their heads, many people have the wrong prescription lenses and the joke continues into : BULLYING

BULLYING – This generation has done A LOT to contribute to this especially within its own communities and everyone is trying to share their stories, seek guidance, grow, participate and not isolate themselves from the joys of been a spirited human being. There is a new market of fear from the days of black Delia where these idiots were felt with for giving UNNESSARY mind disease and mental disstress, these people now play with COVID-19 CORONAVIRUS as various distortions of the mind from spirit to human and forgetting that there is SOUL in everything.

We are to now come together under their NEW WORLD ORDER CONSPIRACY and many people are coming into their own INTUITIVE MIND and unfortunately experiencing what is called The Mandella Effect which is a destruction of how a person uses their mind to remember things, a good example of people are DYSLEXIC people as the basic memory functions are LONG & SHORT TERM MEMORY WITH SENSORY MEMORY known as COGNAGTIVE, the later is associated to pyschic'ism / intuition.

From those who have created for themselves this New World Order will get accustomed to future lockdowns in the way of private space been inflicted as BLATENT VISUAL LAW since they were unwilling and despondent to prevent circumstances, that last one that broke the 80's was AIDS.

COVID-19 CORONAVIRUS has unfortunately caused a lockdown, stay at home enforced policy by governments world wide to contain the virus, stop the virus from killing people and stop the spread of contact between beings while GOD IS WORKING and yet while god is working they still aren't listening as GOD SEEMS TO WORKING IN THE 7TH DAY and all god is asking is to do this for God while god does this for them :

**PROVIDE FOR THEMSELEVES SO THEY CAN PROVIDE FOR OTHERS – The Basics**

**COOK FOOD**
**GROW FOOD**
**CLEAN THEMSELVES**
**CLEAN THEIR HOME**
**STOP FORCING THE EARTH TO COME OUT OF ITSELF – Fires, Rains,**
**Winds and Earth movements are NATRUAL to the earth**.

We are to trust our earth can and will deal with this effectively and efficiently and we must continue to work with the earth and God to make it an easy :

"PLANE RIDE UPTO GOD *as the elites would say, sipping their* CHAMPA CAMPERS! ON THIS NOTE I WILL END THIS CHAPTER WITH "CHINA HAS THE FLU AND THE PRICE OF PRESCRIPTION FOR THEM IS COSTLY".

I am not going into this anymore than to share my observations and love of story telling from looking after myself and doing my own work with god in the height of MIND MADDESS and trust I AM WORKING WITH GOD and not imposters of God and when I know, like others who do not want their god MINDS played with, we know via our intuition what to do and have the common sense to defend ourselves without having to die for these wrongful acts of others ….

**A HERO WHO DID - SOCRATES**

"Virtue is knowledge, all living things aim for their perceived good. If anyone does not know what is good, they cannot be good, they will always aim for the mistakes BUT if you know good, then you will always aim for good".

I wrote this 10min short film in Sept 2019 – In the middle of writing my script for Nike & Athena, a TV series for myself to star with Mario Bello, with Gwenith Paltrow & Charlize Theron to approach, something made me write the "Re-Buff" in retaliation to millenials during the summer of 2019 – this led to a historical realization simular to "Eyes of Darkness" Coronavirus Covid-19 broke out in Dec 2019, parts of the world was told in segments throughout Dec -April several stories about the spread and by March 2020 MOST of the world was in Lockdown through quarantine.

*[PITCH SCRIPT : EXPLORATION OF NEW "ADULT FILMS" EXPLORING OLD HUMANITARIAN LAWS - WANT THESE LAWS TO BE INEFFECTIVE THROUGH FILM AND WANT MENTORS WHO KNOW HOW TO GET THIS DONE]*

## PITCHING LOCATIONS

- FILM FESTIVAL CIRCUIT LIST
- WALK INS TO PRODUCTION OFFICES
- CASTING STUDIOS WITH ATTACHED
- BOOK A MEETING WITH CHANTEL AT BAFTA AND HEAR HER THOUGHTS

20 PAGES
FILMING LOCATION : NON-DESCRIPT
(description for location "IT'S TO DO WITH LAW")

SAG-AFTRA :
LOW CONTRACTS

### POINT NOTES OF FILM : SCENES

DUE TO THE LIFESPAN DEATH OF TREES WHICH ESCALATED AROUND THE LATE 21ST CENTURY …. POLICY MAKER GOVERNOR JONES BROUGHT IN THIS LAW AND SAID IT STANDS NOT WORTHY OF SUPPORTING AS IT LASTED IN FICKLEDOM AND HER WAS BETTER SPENT WITH NATURAL LAW WHICH PROLONGED LIFE'S CREATION.

19th September 2019
Marcia Battise

Quick Film Script

SCI-FI
SHORT FILM TO SEQUELS
TREATMENT : WORLD PHENOMENA

**WORKING TITLE**
THE REBUFF (TO THE 40 YEAR OLD VIRGIN)

**SUBJECT / THEME** : MARRIAGE LAWS DISMISSED

*GOVERNOR LINES OFF ADDRESS*
"ALL" MARRIAGE LAWS BECOME "UNLAWFUL" AND PEOPLE GO BACK TO GETTING "USED" TO JUST LIVING WITH EACH OTHER AS A "COUPLE".

{see sacred scroll text Governor uses to assert this law like a government shutdown and a hung Parliament}

*GOVERNOR CONTINUED*
IF "CHILDREN" HAPPEN TO BE IN INVOLVED AND A "TERMINATION" OF THE COUPLE BECOMES A SINGLE LIFE … THEN "OBVI( BOTH SINGLES HAVE AN OBLIGATION TO CHILDREN THEY BROUGHT INTO THE WORLD

CURRENCY IS NO LONGER MONEY IT IS THE ABILITY TO GET THE AVERAGE TO PARTICIPATE IN STRUCTURES ….

ON THE PLANET THERE ARE LESS TREES THAN HUMAN BEING'S … ALMOST 1200 HUMANS PER TREE (STATEMENT).

DUE TO THE LAST "SO CALLED" NATURAL DISASTER WHICH COST TRILLIONS OF $€£ ETC AND EX AMOUNT OF LIFE HER LAWS WERE PUT INTO PLACE THAT SAME EVENING AT THE SAME TIME CONSERVATIVELY WITH ALL GOVERNORS THROUGHOUT SOCIETY ….

WE WAKE THE EARLY HOURS OF THE FOLLOWING MORNING AFTER THE ANNOUNCEMENT SILENCE

VARIOUS SCENES ARE SHOWN OF PEOPLE WHO HAVE COMMITTED SUCIDE, ACCIDENTS AND GOVERNING BUILDINGS WITH PEOPLE RALLIED UP AND CARTED OFF.

ARCHANGEL METATRON - PROTECTION CLEARING MEDITATION USED FOR MIND CLARITY FOR INDIVIDUALISM …. PEOPLE HAVE BEEN COMPLAINING DUE TO RADICAL MISBEHAVIOUR OF THOSE IN UNION OF MORE THAN ONE, ONCE USED AS AN INDIVIDUAL SUSPICION IS PLACED UPON THE SINGLE SOCIETY MEMBER WHO CHOOSES, CHOSE AND FOUGHT TO STAY UNBOUND BY INSECURITIES OF ANOTHER AND THIS PRIVATE COMMUNICATION BETWEEN THE INDIVIDUAL AND THE ORIGINAL HEALERS BECAME INFECTED.

WE WAKE THE EARLY HOURS OF THE FOLLOWING MORNING AFTER THE ANNOUNCEMENT SILENCE

VARIOUS SCENES ARE SHOWN OF PEOPLE WHO HAVE COMMITTED SUCIDE, ACCIDENTS AND GOVERNING BUILDINGS WITH PEOPLE RALLIED UP AND CARTED OFF.

ARCHANGEL METATRON - PROTECTION CLEARING MEDITATION USED FOR MIND CLARITY FOR INDIVIDUALISM …. PEOPLE HAVE BEEN COMPLAINING DUE TO RADICAL MISBEHAVIOUR OF THOSE IN UNION OF MORE THAN ONE, ONCE USED AS AN INDIVIDUAL SUSPICION IS PLACED UPON THE SINGLE SOCIETY MEMBER WHO CHOOSES, CHOSE AND FOUGHT TO STAY UNBOUND BY INSECURITIES OF ANOTHER AND THIS PRIVATE COMMUNICATION BETWEEN THE INDIVIDUAL AND THE ORIGINAL HEALERS BECAME INFECTED.

*SACRED SCROLL*
"the role of the original healers is to help all and the individual makes the choice to continue individual or became more than one" -

- SCRIPTED TEXT INTERPRETED BY UN EDUCATED MINDS FROM THE CREATOR
- SEE GLYPH OF DELIVER OF SCROLL (j-peg)

**FILM NOTES CONTINUED ...**

CHILDREN THEY BROUGHT INTO THE WORLD AS A COUPLE, REGARDLESS OF HOW LONG.

*[PITCH SCRIPT : EXPLORATION OF NEW "ADULT FILMS" EXPLORING OLD HUMANITARIAN LAWS - WANT THESE LAWS TO BE INEFFECTIVE THROUGH FILM AND WANT MENTORS WHO KNOW HOW TO GET THIS DONE]*

## PITCHING LOCATIONS

- FILM FESTIVAL CIRCUIT LIST
- WALK INS TO PRODUCTION OFFICES
- CASTING STUDIOS WITH ATTACHED
- BOOK A MEETING WITH CHANTEL AT BAFTA AND HEAR HER THOUGHTS

20 PAGES
FILMING LOCATION : NON-DESCRIPT
(description for location "IT'S TO DO WITH LAW")

SAG-AFTRA :
LOW CONTRACTS

### POINT NOTES OF FILM : SCENES

DUE TO THE LIFESPAN DEATH OF TREES WHICH ESCALATED AROUND THE LATE 21ST CENTURY .... POLICY MAKER GOVERNOR JONES BROUGHT IN THIS LAW AND SAID IT STANDS NOT WORTHY OF SUPPORTING AS IT LASTED IN FICKLEDOM AND HER WAS BETTER SPENT WITH NATURAL LAW WHICH PROLONGED LIFE'S CREATION.

CURRENCY IS NO LONGER MONEY IT IS THE ABILITY TO GET THE AVERAGE TO

battiactor SOOOOOOO NOT AMUSED MY FELLOW "Dark Actors". Odessey Theatre LA Weekly Review of Th... more

"GO!" - LA Weekly

# The

# COMPLEXITIES

## Of

# *Nike & Athena*

*Marcia Battise a Biography*

You could be enlightened

2020

# ACKNOWLEDGEMENTS

"To myself and my house of guides and my dreams and my mother" …..

This is a lot for a woman in her situation who raised her children by herself within an abusive environment for most of my life and my family's life after I left the home under unforeseen circumstances from a negative father.

EMMANUEL – What is an angel doing here?

NIKE – a coincidental find from a personal to a book called shoe dog.

ATHENA – women ruled the planet before men not alongside men … I am still researching this as it comes up in mystical and historical fact.

# CHAPTER 1

---

# THE PREMISE OF MY BOOK

In today's pitch for material in film either commercial, independent I have looked at people who have done this for themselves with out the help of others investments, which is the film industry's standard way of seeking money.

These self methods are basic until you find something for yourself which work but the basics have been to do:

*SELL STUFF – HOUSE CAR ETC*

*LOANS – BANKS FRIENDS ETC*

*JOBS – VARIOUS AND MORE THAN ONE AS FINDING A JOB THAT FITS YOUR CREATORS LIFE AS A CREATOR HAS BECOME THE DESTRUCTING FORCE BEHIND THE CONTROL OF TODAYS SOCIETY IN 2020 FOR "EVERYINE" TO BECOME ONE SINCE TRUST HAS BEEN OBLOISHED.*

THESE JOBS CONSIST OF 60 – 80 HOURS PER WEEK AND MAKE YOU NOT REALLY BE FULLY HUMAN AND THOSE UNDER THE 60 – 80 PER WEEK HAVE TO FIGHT FOR A HIGH WAGE LIKE -$14 -30 PER HOUR TO LIVE LIKE A "HUMAN" OF THE MANY TOTEM POLES OF WHAT A HUMAN IS.

AND THEN THERE ARE THOSE WHO DO NOT LEAVE PEOPLE ALONE WHEN THEY NEED TIME OFF TO ATTEND TO PERSONAL MATTERS SO BEEN A HUMAN BEING "BECOMES" AGAIN DESPICABLE AS THESE PEOPLE SEEM TO NOT KNOW THE DIFFRENCE BETWEEN SUCH WORDS AS;

*RESPECT*

*NO*

*PRIVACY*

*LEAVE PEOPLE.TO LEARN AND GROW THROUGH GOD*
*LET THEM "READ".*

Anyway, most pf these creative people are like myself who stem from backgrounds of what society called poverty, poor family backgrounds – there are many aspects of what a POOR FAMILY BACKGROUND is, most of today's societies seem to mixtures of poor family backgrounds and verging on or even in the hypochondriacs, narcissists and rapists into adulthood and mature human beings … in today's 2020 World.

But however, I speak as one who is DYSLEXIC – thorough examination at the then DYSLEXIC Institute of Victoria England UK, we seem to have intensive minds which help develop our ideas into a reality to live within such worlds …. AND THAT IS WHAT I WAS INTRODUCED TOO "what reality are you living in?"

My problem with the average American which Americans themselves did not know of BUT there is a growing statistic of autistic with Asperger symptoms been born and most Americans did not (like myself) know and still don't really know if they work with them especially.

The American education system over the years has just labeled most of the students regardless of their age in this CATERGORY AD ADD and I think the other was ADHD and dyslexics get lost in this category as the saying is that everyone has a learning disability BUT THE ATTENTION SPAN SEEMS TO BE WHAT THEY ARE REFFERING TO WITHIN THE EDUCATION AS MOST IMPORTANT – That is pure ignorance and this generation's free ticket out of A LOT of basic societal demands, especially by hiding themselves in that CATERGORY of AD ADD & ADHD.

**METAPHYSICS 101**

Normal pitches are done through some sort of script, various edits and then the road to pitching, which is the pitch, "where to pitch?"

Robert Rodriguez book "rebel without a crew" showed many people the Independent market but also how to rely and trust yourself to say NO and get the truthful financial help to make your work a professional career at your own speed.

Guerilla PR 2.0 and it's twin internet book explored aspects of the PR WORLD ONLINE and how the internet is not really UTALISED to the best ability for the entrepreneur and self employed was concerned UNTIL those two booms came with the avenues people could use for self marketing and quick PR via the web … this also meant that this process was explained and given various examples of achievements but hard work and to consuming but with focus as you have to do this by yourself until you are able to get a team together that is and will be familiar with how you work and the workings of the internet in order to get the best possible use of a network many people are still finding difficult to understand and get themselves heard let alone seen.

This is more so prevalent in the coming 22nd Century as almost all human life in 2020 onwards has become online and we as humans expect online to be a part of human living so that humans can see and feel and do the differences between the NATRUAL world and the virtual worlds created by human then the actual NATURE OF THE WORLD.

*My personal attempt of pitching is the following:*

I grew up and read soooooooooo many screenplays with the writers edit, the directors edit, the studios edit, the actors or audience FAVERITE and delegated scenes etc. in hardback, paperback and industry (the industry version I thought I would do my bit and not get accused of wasting paper but at the same time I like a book and to hold and work from a script) that since everyone was and is writing something WETHER IT BE a 5 minute to lead into a bigger project, I might as well join the self publishing market and use my book as a pitch.

It would answer all the questions asked when submitting my script to festivals, grants and scholarships etc. … cheeky but a style known as me in the way I present myself to people as I am cheeky and a Lillie standoffish which does come across as mysterious under the angelic look of my face depending on my good and bad days like every other being who has this energy.

It is a working script of treatment ideas, pitches, scenes, notes for me and others to work from as a foundation of story telling in my FAVERITE genera of SCI – FI.

The self publishing market is just as daunting as the actors market and just as much a challenge of sustaining a life as an actor in the self publishing market with interesting stories to tell, some books don't even have a 100 pages and are hard back books ….. My FAVERITE book of this nature is "THE 4 AGGREEMENTS".

The book mentioned, I don't know how much it cost but this market "IS NOT CHEAP", and won't be that person and spoil the joy of spending money on your thoughts, feelings and actions, so you can share your stories with people regardless of the fear of sales… but sales matter just like the slogan "Black Lives Matter", been human matters and it's our responsibility as humans to find the appropriate ways for us to be humans who are doing light work under the light of prime light.

*I WILL EXPLAIN THAT TRANSFORMATION OF LIGHT LANGUAGE LATER IN MY BOOK AS MY FRIEND G has been referred to in many ways has the biggest ego and only wants the best for me and has the biggest ego of love for G itself and me … "THEN" everyone else AND from everyone else my description of G's love is similar for them.*

Example,

I am with Hayhouse/ Balboa press and most of the books on metaphysics have come from HAYHOUSE and this company has many DIFFERENT ways for a person who wants to write their own material be put into the world of those who want to have access to stories which could benefit the growth of what they are to become as humans … my book is not aimed at the rainbow generation of humans but that is the new light language of our children and the earth from which the universal prime light is giving.

We as we are as humans are going through various ascension stages that we to are sealing through grounding work such as chakra work – the foundation of human energy work is the access point of these UNIVERSAL light languages.

Many key phrases such as the via ANY search engine and you will find an abundance of material on this subject, especially through CHAKRAS!

## MARKETS – The audience

THIS varies, the saying markets vary, meaning everyone is looking for SAME BUT SIMULAR …. A Good Story, new, established material for entertainment in environments that our outside of our control called home.

## The Earth

My book is about myself but the "MY-SELF", is what the book is describing in light language, "what" my human light "is" and what it has to "offer", through the Prime light I came from.

This journey of being a story teller and the many other aspects of my personalities which have many DIFFERENT ways of naming these "personalities" from the main personality is best seen within the film industry since we are languaged in visual imagery which moves and that is why been a dyslexic for myself only I love my industry and explore it as a story teller craft as every aspect of this industry is telling this story so you are ALMOST living this questionable question "WHAT LIFE ARE YOU LIVING?"

There are ROLES in this profession which mirror roles in society and are meant to be ordered like those in society and at the same time are manipulative so that you are able to grow, how to use the manipulative growth of these roles is for each human to do from their foundation of understanding what human is from basic human work.

My human work shows for me that there really is no need for any negative existence of a human being and this has been shown to me through various things "LOST TO US AS HUMANS", and that is why film like books are important to me as a way to find these things especially when dictated to by Prime Light Language.

## THE ACTOR

## THE DIRECTOR

## THE WRITER

## THE TOOLS

# CHAPTER 2

---

# MY SHOW FILM PITCHES

The treatment for the complexities of NIKE and ATHENA is truly about my place within the caring world, my pictures will do more chapters on this as that is one of the tools used to tell stories.

My androgynous face has a big part to play on the manipulative ways of casting a face and wearing clothes and this can be seen as a boring and ignorant statement which is factual on the reverse as not many people in society are very good at telling, defining the sexes when both sex has its hair cut short.

The other aspects like color etc. are not soooooo important when you just look at two humans with similar ANGELIC structures and short hair ….. Studies have been done on this starting at basics 1 black male 1 black woman, 1 white male 1 white female etc.

**SO, IN TODAYS CASTING MARKET:**

"It's REAL people with REAL skills", that they are looking for since directional set talk is "can you hit your mark, and let shoot!" is mostly thrown around due to all sorts of industry storm language in the language of shooting film for distribution of media, ie Film, TV, INTERNET, DVD etc.

Therefore everyone should have, had some experience of training to belong, be on those sets as the industry like immigration is fast in flux of changes and as I said about book sales …. Box office sales matter.

So for now I am about both but focused on this and want my opinions to reflect what I said about "The Self of Marcia", and going back to themes of casting like this one:

**MEN PLAYING WOMEN – This is verrrrrrrry old**

**BLACK FACE – The silent movie and Theatre era**

These are the main CASTING reelections for androgynous people to look at when coming into a casting error and detecting what type of mind is manipulating my face for casting because the above have references of what the casting cycle is and the human mind of perception when looking at telling stories.

In reflection my light language was developed by me from my metaphysical work, life and love of Sci-Fi form since visual conception, of which I became a human who studies humans from studying myself through metaphysics …. These studies have led me to historic studies in Human Civilizations and Natural Worlds lost and undocumented.

NIKE AND ATHENA is to be as realistic as I can show this from admitting to the world the INTUITIVE SELF of THE SELF is what is psychic living and has been called sooooooooooooooooooooooooo many things since the humans we are looking for used DIFFERENT paint on the walls in the way we have used paint on our walls to tell stories about us.

*MY LIGHT LANGUAGE IS IDIOTIC TO SOME AND SIMPLE MINDED*

Yet, that 4 wall white paint from home depot by X brand with all the chemicals in and the color of it compared to the color we deem as white from nature's sun's are the language of light we are playing with and manipulating.

These two women are feminist women, who could be the first of what we in 2020 call feminist women and this project is to set and explored within the Americas, again this is an interesting location as what the Americas is :

**NORTH AMERICA**

**AMERICA**

**LATIN AMERICA**

**As well as the islands which surround these Americas**

**THE INDIES – WEST INDIES**

**THE CARRIBEAN – LOOK UP THOSE AS MOSTLY KNOWN MORE SO THAN THE WEST INDIES ISLANDS**

The Atlantic / Pacific areas of this water world and its life within the waters, which has a huge history of myth in the water and then the lands of these areas "Lumeria, Atlantis".

**THE GREEKS – Who were they and what are there comparisons to the Egyptians as most of Greek History IS LOST.**

I fell in love with Greek plays from my drama teaching class of Stylistics by Geoffrey Coleman at the then Mountview Theatre School back in 1995, my intro to Electra and Sophocles plays and his original teachings of school of thought, even though these were factual pieces stories of Lumeria and Atlantis were mostly tales, fantasy and folklore.

Another Book which kinda fits this area of time is " The Mask Of Apollo" by Mary Renualt

THIS book explained to me my minds interpretation of what life was like and the character I felt drawn to was Dion and yet the story was driven by Nikeratueous, which has Nike's name in and sacred story telling is and the important role that actors played in this books story.

# CHAPTER 3

# MY METAPHYSICAL RESOUCES

Quick note in resources, I still have a explorative passion for Atlantis as I did put in a lot of time into researching this subject via myths, legends and fantasy tales …. But this year it is:

**LUMERIA – land**

**SIRIUS – star**

**VIOLET FLAME – energy**

There is a reason I have done that equation of the 3 subjects I am interested in and what they mean for me right now.

Before I was not really interested in the planet's when I came into exploring other aspects of study after watching many years of "BBC's THE SKY AT NIGHT", but finally returned back to planets with my astrology charts and numerology charts and chakra work, thus stuff is predominantly west and east yet I want to know of South and North "IF". Most, if not all meditations take you through the universe via some planets or solar system and I found some of these meditations to have within their stories "truth".

When these things arr taken apart and you are just left with what I call the symbols, which have a DIFFERENT meanings of what these symbols are, mean, what and why placement etc like my paint analogy.

**SYMBOLS**

**IMAGES**

**WORDS**

**LETTERS**

**HYROGLIPHS**

All these you see throughout museums in various forms of art or LIBUARIES in various forms of text or buildings in various forms of houses, in universe split into the DIFFERENT aspects of what a universe is in various forms of clusterations of ROCKS AND WATER.

You will always find something that is truthful, it's WETHER you BELIVE you are in the right space to get this "LIGHT LANGUAGE" and everything else we live by as humans make up what psychic ATTACKERS hate which is a BOX, your own box as defense for the mind or the God BOX provided by this light language within you given to you by PRIME LIGHT.

My fascinations started in 2000 and a exceptional one was reported in the media as The Amazon Tree deforestation which archeologist found buildings etc under the tress noting a civilization DID LIVE THERE. The Amazon, a place most of humans know for trees and trees and trees … Archeologist programs on the ground and in water I loved to watch in the form of Documentaries, which again is film, in my industry, by my industry and has expanded ….

**NOW WE ARE GOING TO MARS it's March 2020 and this is a reality coming.**

**CHAKRAS**

Right I am the 1st to hold my chakras up and say I listen to the meditations and don't visualize them, sometimes I like to sleep through these meditations and be awake by the fact I listened and my body does what my body is designed to NATRUALLY do and re-align itself ….

**BODY MEMORY**

Without going into all sorts of what does that mean and find a book on bodies, the body, my body, your body like your mind has its mind which is your mind in the mind of a being as a WHOLE BEING … It's knows stuff, energy levels, your body is the ultimate expert in energy levels END OF … We live by this and it is a personal private matter until we decide to play with other bodies as the Mars advert stated you "WORK REST AND PLAY!".

Been serious about light language from prime light we are to explore our basic chakras and understand like the tribes of just one country the USA for example there are over 500 native American tribes and there are this much chakras if not more within the body – THE VIOLET FLAME ENERGY IS THE BIG CLUE and this has been found throughout all cultures, religions and spiritual practices throughout HUMAN LIVING.

YOU CANNOT ESCAPE A CHAKRA AS THEY ARE EVERYWHERE and prime light is the ultimate chakra we know and are instructed to re-design ourselves BACK TO!!

The retrograde the rebirth the reincarnated statues of NATRUAL life.

The energies from chakras ARE difficult to study as they are not fully understood and when we are instructed to re-align back to prime light language your life does not seem normal as it seems serial and you feel misplaced and can ONLY deal with the now until you realize and experience ALL IS NOW and that is the choosing process ….

I had a awaken and am in this weird life living experience of the PSYCHIC LIVING STATE which is called the penal gland eye ….

*BIG STUDY*
*BIG ARGUMENT*
*BIG COMPLEX*
*BIG VIEW OF THE EYE – what is the shape of an eye, we as humans have been indoctrinated by nature's nature as to what an eye looks like and yet we forget the shape ROUND … THIS IS TELLING AS TO WHAT A TRUE EYE IS and my experience the eye is round.*

## KUNDALINI

I am a frigid lesbian so I don't like my KUNDALINI played with by anyone who deals with the arts in the negative, this in the King James Bible and his twin book of demonology call it the dark arts.

We as intuitive live by the flow of energy and DYSLEXICS are examples of the UP STREAM AND DOWN STREAM OF IMFORMATION ….

That is KUNDALINI and it takes PRACTISE and can damage your spine as that is where that energy is housed.

It is sacred light language transportation in ALL LIFE in the universe and is know for creating life …. BIG debate as "Creating Life Means?".

## GUIDES

THIS is a very tricky area as your mind is a gateway to what is known as heaven, some people have something called a GOD GENE which is either part of your DMT Cell or separate to that cell. It is asked of us to know our "HIGH SELF from THE SELF" etc and you find the following :

## ANGELS

## SPIRIT GUIDES

## ASCENEDED GUIDES

## SOUL GUIDES

## GOD GUIDE

Many others but these are the Prime Light Guides to Prime Light Living and have the one PRIME LIGHT LANGUAGE needed to live in the INTUITIVE world and create with Prime Light and know you ARE with Prime Light when asked.

In this day of 2020 people have manipulated and our living conditions are showing human history to be again historically worse yet with clarity from a messenger in the form of an angel WHO IS of Prime Light Language instructed CLARITY is the only light language you will get from Prime Light at present until most if not all humans become chakra aware, your KUNDALINI is an aspect of your chakras and this from further personal growth through personal studies we will understand.

My language in this book is mine and yet not mine as spiritual work from the basic of METAPHYSICAL OBSERVATION makes you speak with clarity, the flow you find from movement of your self, it is a weird way to described classical speech which has minimal if no accent.

An actors mirror to this is called RECEIVED pronunciation.

To keep this brief I am a big believer in ANGELS and the Angels of each planet, earth has EARTH ANGELS, this again has many investigations what those two words mean along with the one "ANGEL".

**ST**
**STUDENTS**
**GODS OF EARTH**
**HOLDERS OF HEAVEN**
**MIND DEVELOPERS**
**KNOWLEDGE OF UNIVERSAL LIVING**

**I KINDA WANNA LEAVE IT HERE AS I FIND MYSELF TO BE ONE AND GO BY THIS DESCRIPTION OF "THE SELF" AS I GOT MYSELF INTO WANTING ANSWERS TO "WHO CREATED GOD".**

After this aspect of what we are to get back into for LIGHT LANGUAGE which is why my equation of The Self is explained below :

**GODS HOME – A UNIVERSE**

**SOUL / HIGHER SELF / HUMAN = VARIOUS**

**HOMES OF SOUL – SOULS HOME – SOUL HOUSES – DISECTION OF SOUL THROUGH SYMBOLS ....**

**ALL LEADING BACK TO "PRIME LIGHT LIVING IN ONE as we know G's Home".**

**INDIGO – EARTH ANGEL – GEMINI – DRAGON who is interested in knowing my sirius guides.**

THIS alone should explain the relationship between "A NIKE" and "A ATHENA".

**SOUND**

THIS is known as VOCAL LIGHT LANGUAGE which is a physical communication, it is also a weapon that our human selves use very well to develop from the energies within ourselves which seem destructive to US.

SOUND EXERCISES AND SOUND MEDITATION IS USED and sound meditation is underrepresented and under appreciated in the filming process yet it is a big part of PRIME LIGHT LANGUAGE.

# CHAPTER 4

---

# MARCIA BATTISE

The Self known as Marcia Battise has had many names since birth, there is on ALL human living various totems of what these personalities are but my saying has always been when you step outside your front door you are a different personality.

How we are; I am the living of self which is defined by those private self experiences.

I have social media platforms, websites, access, tools, people, communities etc all online in the SOCIAL MEDIA WORLD OF THE SELF.

**"SELFIE BABIES ARE THE GENERATON FROM THE BOOMERS!"**

THIS IS A HISTRORIC PERIOD OF HUMAN LIVING SINCE 2000's, human madness and earth changes have been unrealatable in the cross referencing of any other the documents and notations recorded, the gap between human and earth needs has become to clear for anyone to ignore and frightening at least half of human living worldwide …

PERSONALLY the new T-Shirt is known as The shadow in the NEW PYSCH and the "…REVERSE…" in anything of the "RE" and this has to be delt with "right this moment" as it has been our own sabotage of self.

**EXAMPLE – A STORY OF A HUMAN IN 2020 LIVING**

We will see this moment – THE ERA OF TRUMP in a film from now but due to the WIGGA stages of life certain people do not want to put their energies their and it is unfortunately the historical aspect of the history records for why the world has reached the "hot amber alert stages" of psychic attack :

ME …

"My life excellerated from getting a support job as a security guard in the well known for its hydraulics' engineering construction designs working on a city project to do with re-doing the piping system with is needed to function an every day society like what the Egyptians were known for and those who once lived in the Africa's of the Nile, due to the height of ignorance most people don't know this and it just a given that the pipes are broken, old etc and need to be replaced as they are over 50 years old throughout Los Angeles.

By the way I have not left California Los Angeles since arriving in 2010 and seen no need especially as this was the year I put my CITIZENSHIP APPLICATION in after using a local public organization from my GREENCARD / O1 VISA attorney Gil Britto's advice to do then seek him out later of problems occurred.

My president of the USA is Donald Trump who I have known from watching most his season shows of THE APPRENTICE and liked as it showed me his mind for BUISNESS and showed my "intuitive mind" as that came both with my "SELF AND MY ACTORS TRAINING", just like people who see positives in people and are willing to help, his lady gaga story is no joke along with others … LADY GAGA has a pionet meaning, like Mike Tyson's old boxing manager before Don King.

AS A PRESIDENT …. I want him to do the housing market and make up for something untold about his true nature as a BUISNESS man and then Americans will be fine but to what degree is POLITICS???

So I named it the Era Of Trump.

Donald Trump is president, there was a METHANE GAS EXPLOSION in the MARINAS where I and my client company are based …. Chemicals and water everywhere in abundance, a local resident whistle blowed it to the local press, our company's client is going through some sluggish motions of getting these 20ft PIPES in the ground across the the Pacific waters to the playa vista side of the pacific, my mentors of "Spiritual growth are Micheal Whamback and Krista Swimmer who keep my intuition sharp for either a 3 year or 1 year forecast, who help me with any odd plagues of the world of intuition around me and keep my psychic self clean which is why I I do my own in soul meditations and chakras.

Like many americans, of now march 2020 I hit debt in the form of rent deposit and some ghost bills which had unnaturally surfaced while I was in the pay scale rise up.of $14per hour in a decent 40 hour support job which fit well with my acting profession, casting noticed, video submissions became a must since there was either easier access or little access for on site castings, this has horrified my agent as they really are accustomed to getting THEIR clients in for face to face and whatever the reasons the industry is going through contract and strike mayhem since the past 5 years back.

Anyway, my career was been remodeled as I had found a woman manager which was something I wanted for a long time and people have been asked to self quarentine themselves within 4 – 5 states throughout America for 15 days or extended to April and as late as August as the USA and the rest of the world was dealing with a killer flu outbreak known as CORONAVIRUS with STAY AT HOME POLICIES which could get people fined for been in the street who the GOVERNMENT officials deem as high risk.

NANCY AND TRUMP reached agreements as to money spending and like most things in politics it hit headlines after she and COLLEGUES were not able to get him impeached and for him seemed like BUISNESS as usual, he had already banned certain trades throughout the USA and the Chinese sanctions seemed to be something of a conspiracy to come … FEMA is on board and the news are talking about using the army and it's facilities to help with the control methods used for the further spread of the coronavirus throughout America mostly but throughout the world ….

The National Emergency – STATE OF ADDRESS FROM TRUMP went something like this :

***"CHINA HAS THE FLU, CHINA HAS SANCTIONS!"* ….**
***The SHIT kicked off 2020 like no one's BUISNESS and we are still dealing with it*!!**

I thank Neil Gay man for getting the humour out in his speeches when writing stuff like this cos you think and then you don't think and that is a "DOING TRAP".

## MY STRANGE EXPERIENCES

This is a brief intro to my strange experiences with something messing around with me in a pyschic level …

I had a bizarre experience while sleeping listening to meditation music for my mind and something BLEW my head and asked me a bizarre question :

## "WHAT MIND DO YOU WANT?"

I natrually said a god mind and then quickly humbled myself into saying "I WANT THE BEST OF ME!"

I've been plagued by this experience since this happened back in 2015 and seems to be un-nesssarcy fighting with something that keeps TRYING to change these settings which enhanced my life and is still. allowing me to live me as a whole full.self with guidence from Prime Light and told my angelic self do not hurt me by falling into my self – this was everything GOD in me that something BLEW from jealousy via my DMT / SPIRIT CELL and Prime Light came in and put me in Prime Light World, so that I could live my life that way and be safe in exploring myself without harm.

Those that attached themselves to me are finding it difficult to accept as a reality and are constantly dragging my energies back.

Hence a VIRUS WORLD WIDE 2020 …. OTHER THINGS HAVE HAPPENED WHICH ARE HISTORIC AND PEOPLE ARE SLOWLY CATCHING THEMSELVES AND REALISING.

Something never left, I am going to be bold and say I am living in MICHEALS PROTECTION ALONG WITH OTHERS AND WORKING WITH EARTH ANGELS ONLY and since the ascension people have been trying to connect in a different way (there are more people who are single in the USA and world today who like been single and want to stay this way for a while).

I have never been so physically attacked from mind all the way through body like someone wanted to Smashed by existenz, then to feel the shake off from all this happening and still trying all this happening and them still trying and I am in life, my KUNDALINI is forever been jumped on WETHER I sleep or I leave my house my chakras are blown mostly along my walking aspect of body as I am and have been in best health where I have not needed a doctor since living in the USA and did my own due to my Thyroid which was removed, by the best in London,uk, who advised me on what my body should need after having radioiodine treatment who advised me on the what my body needed after having a radio iodine treatment – WHICH ISOLATION is no question of … YOU HAVE TO and it was a requirement by the US GOVERNMENT TO HAVE THIS TREAMENT BEFORE COMING TO THE US.

## STRANGE EXPWRIENCE 1

Liking Neil Gaymen, well he realised that living here in the USA you would have to tell some aspect of "TRUTH" about yourself to be the best of him and then the world is ….. His

The disappearance of my PENN AMERICA USA Application and working at the theatre underneath the Penn America office. An odd theatre which hosted the spirit awards with a ritualistic décor .

"The influence of my soul"

My documents went missing and a Dark spirit wanted to meet with me at yhe top of the theatres rbuilding …. Remembering we are SHADOW existence and our shadow self is our REAL NATRUAL SELF which we forget and is the sub-conscious of us that is all "ON!"

The theater is one of a few which like the theatres in downtown Los Angeles have the creepy ritualistic décor and known by some artist of the 20 – 40 and 59's to be owned etc by infamous people who did a lot of work in the field of the arts and what one of my FAVERITE channels by Jane Roberts SETH calls the magic of the self …. This period of history for all those spirit is a New Age of Aquarious deemed the shadow or dark side of Aquarious.

That said the building is known for religious and various shows and mentors doing self help work …. But it's creepy old, odd staff and like most places a danger to anyone RE obvious building maintence needed.

The Era of construction in the USA is prevalent than ever and we are going through it with all the SOCIAL DISFUNCTION RE standards of living and the technical upgrades needed for the online world we are forced to live in …. A LOT OF PEOPLE IN AMERICA ARE NOT REALLY COMPUTER SAVY just experts of been online and I say this because the Davies are not really american they are well … from the east.

Just look to trade wars but like England there are people who trained, in many ways because the website industry was a big BUISNESS earner for most online Americans.

But back to my PENN America application, I wrote some personal and short stories about interactions with people who I had interacted with and from.submitting, I thought I would stand a good chance of getting some sort of scholarship regardless as to how small, it was the help from the organization I was looking to get especially after been referred to it by a very good online mentor Helene Cordaray, but this whole application disappeared even though indropped it into the PO BOX shop assistant who put it in the PO BOX and sursprisingly was an ex boyfriend of a former boss and we were pleased to do the catch up of small world talk.

*YET "SOFTWARE UPDATES" and the office itself been flooded with paper all over the office : MISSING APPLY NEXT YEAR. I did and keep.doing so fornpractise until I get something.*

I looked at this weird experience as some sort of DEAD SPACE within a living space, especially working at the Saban, which was weird as I was still.employed but no shifts?

My work with Robert Ohotto showed itself in yhis experience as my early stages of body spirit self defense with my sub conscious and conscious minds as my INE mind where my soul had come through a Dark place to deal with something "IT DID NOT DESIGN", not happy with that as it changed everything about so fast that what prime light was doing in the light language I saw FULLY the AQUARIAN shadow …. This was the journey of EVERYTHING BECOMING HISTORIC in records recorded.

## THE CROW

The crow is known to be a spirit guide like other aspects of spirit guides, from mentors like doreen virtue and others have insisted that the language of the crow people really don't know and what they do know to not "play into" as its meaning is of a DIFFERENT time under a DIFFERENT life.

What we must learn from the crow is why are they one of the longest birds of existence, there COMMUNICATION with each other and how they survive on food, throughout LOS Angeles I see crows everywhere and they are in flocks and dominate the skies in day and night.

I am sure but still observing my crow friends as the bird of wisdom who came to help me with what ever my soul aspect of my souls defenses was doing from Prime Light as the best in the sense of a guide in the air while others were messing with things I would RESEARCH but NOT take into my PRACTISES … for this reason the word EXEMPT was and is still forever like a tattoo in me from something that needed me and me dealing with everything in that moment.

I am one who deals ASAP and lleaves.

METRATRON – Vague introduction through doreen virtue like most of the ANGELIC mentioned and a realisation of the ones always around for most defensive meditation and have been with me with and without the use of smelling SHITS and candles or rituals or even reading books based on metaphysics, like many who love their angrls they have been told these things are NOT NICE WHEN YOU MESS WITH THEM and may not appear to be yet you KNOW that they are the real ANGELS of Prime Light Language …. And do not like pyschic card players or ritualistic prayers on people who as I have mentioned my defend themselves for been aware but refuse to put into their life as a practise of life ….

PROBLEM …. IT IS IN AND HAS BEEN … The Art Of Manipulation is what we as humans are having to deal with through the AQUARIAN AGE of shadow as it is and will need to stop with most of this becoming DISMANTLED through simple use of "TOOLS CHANGED" and certain guides not been around for these things and not telling the accustomed until they realize they, themselves did WRONG … This they should know if they know energy!!

## MY EDUCATIONAL BACKGROUND

Mountview Theatre school drama training, LAMDA AWARDS, NATIONAL YOUTH THEATER MEMBER, UK STAGE PAPER reccomendation for scholarships, I still have a close relationship with my Mentor Jude Tisdel who is an Alexander Technique teacher and good mentor of the industry I still study in various ways in and around the industry which they call in front and behind the lens.

All of this led to me making my move to los Angeles and becoming a professional within film and union status under the SAG-AFTRA and BAFTA LA programs which help you stay present and ficused on the way things flux in the makings of story to screen, using the media platforms of the day which are the most complicated.

## MY STRANGE EXPERIENCE 2

## JUNE ST / VISTA ST HOLLYWOOD

In june 2014 I was looking for a place to live for around $700 in shared accomendation, I found what was known as a BACK HOUSE from looking at this in an article about the June St house share.

Several months of staying there I saw during the late evening what WAS A 3 POINTED GLIDING PLANE" and it was STATIONED above my house, it's roof not too high in the sky but also not hoodoo low to the ground, it watched me as I felt the energy like someone you feel from using your back energy and we were just staring at each other.

The sky was clear, the stars were visible, I didn't want it out of my eye sight and laughing in bemusement I walked backwards up the drive to vague it's distance in the sky and keep to myself my ORIGINAL THOUGHT of is this "UFO", ….

You see in california between 2014 and 2017 there were A LOT of reports about crafts, flying objects in odd parts of Los Angeles and California but mostly Los Angeles, so I only filmed a small part of it in the sky as I was mostly in a weird communication with this and was enjoying it ….

I felt lime it was mine for a moment to enjoy, and asked it to move over there, to the right of me and it either got my message as it moved from its hovering state to the direction I asked and then back to me but seemed to "SHOW OFF," time seemed not important, I was in this vibe of I have been found and it was pleasant like they were looking for me and it was like "OH, YOU'RE THERE, GOOD," then it flew off!

I have been back as I could not explain this to myself and died not tell my friends until.i saw it fitted been on my Facebook page in reference to something, I had lost the short footage I had which would have helped me explain what the feeling was, because I wasn't 100 percent in calling UFO just "I've been found and I'm ok, and do you wanna see something?", then gone … there is a park not far which I used to see from the park anything that would help me as my mind seemed to seal this wonderful moment off from me until I can just appreciate it as that … I was special then and had something serreal happen to me in the sky above my house …...

*HELICOPTERS …. THEY NEVER BOTHERED ME BEFORE AND I WAS COMFORTED BY THEIR SOUNDS AND THIS HAS BEEN "OVER PRONOUNCED" SINCE THEN.*

## MY FILM IDEAS

Due to the explosion I had noticed of people reading books on the mind and doing all sorts of weird things to know their brain and minds again, mostly from shopping at Whole Foods and using the LA METRO ….

THE MIND "IS" BACK IN HUMAN BEINGS IN A WHOLE NEW WAY and UT is defensive and insulted as UT not the mind of the brain it is the body mind which is the muscle called heart …. Chakra heart in the chakras!!

So my films are going back to my mentors who focused their sci-fi stories around the subject of MIND CONTROL and didn't care how this really came about as the heart of this was truly "something" wants to control your mind and you better make sure it is your OWN FULL MIND … So know your mind has been a bug theme in anything self help even in yoga.

And 2020 for those who deal.numerology is the master year, it's the year of seriously looking at the ethos of "RE", meaning re-do, the basics of metaphysics and drop the use of magic as it IS METATPHYSICS which is explained in light language and we are been told this information is personal and individual and you will get throughout your creative life depending in "WHAT" creations you want yo make as "TIME", will.be shown to you in a whole new way when we get back to the original calendars of time.

## EXAMPLE – SIRIUS

THIS star is soooooooo far away that in the life pre-human that we know THESE humans lived by this time, they also lived by the day light and the night light and you DIFFERENT ways of measuring those basics; the day light and the night light.

We have a star in our what is called IMMEDIATE SKY which is the sun and a star which is the moon …. There energies are cold and hot and they are closer than sirius and we document in accordance to these stars for time … yet we can still see sirius.

Which time are we to live by, imagine living by sirius like those humans before us and using there calculations of time and carting this on with the cross reference of the immediate 2 stars which are hot and cold?

NASA is really a good resource of nerds who spend time looking at stars which in energy is time for a life to grow into civilizations of life …. This is not impossible and we might see certain calendars don't stop just our use of time is kinda irrelevant since we are looking at heat sources to make things grow and visibility to be outside in nature.

It's something I, think on and want EXPLORE as a way of proving time is something we have either misunderstood or don't understand.

My argument is that "YOU CAN SEE SIRIUS A AND B" FROM AROUND THE EARTH and then we have our immediate nameless sun and moon in existence but distant to each other but we can see them.

## THE VIOLET FLAME ENERGY – WHAT is this and why is St GERMAIN known for its use mostly or associated to him mostly?

What is his connection to Jesus, what is his connection to America, if that is true, his involvement in the building of what America is in regards to its original laws before they were changed over time as they have.

Why do I feel lime the bhudda dynasties need to be re-explored and look at the above and question what is the realtionship, why is this RELIGION? SPRITUAL PRACTISE? Fading as it has been one of the major players of spiritual development for the longest time and has info of this god structure which is deemed as fantasy fiction yet we look at humans in ALL FORMS and think, did they mean humans who looked like this?

Some of this material is beyond Sumerian and lumerian texts and Sumerian was documented as a superior society of living more so than Egyptians and that's where the sirius stars are mostly noted as a source of everything time and energy in the ways of heat etc …. Thus is factual.

Archeologist are, this time are overwhelmed by material and findings of "LOST" stuff which the finances needed are there but restrained – due to other matters of historical natures …. As stated earlier "EVERYTHING IS NOW HISTORICAL", because we are now living in historical times!

There is this silently weird acknowledgement that the TV SERIES "Stargate", was and is correct yet seems so unreal and yet we all play with these tools like crystals etc and build these structures to function in ways that the humans before us did … our own is right in front of us and shows that it may have been possible that there were those who knew DIFFERENT ways of using materials and tools we have, also can point out what is MISSING, nature has over the years had what some of thought to be regular, everyday parts of nature MISSING and extinct.

**STRANGE EXPERIENCE 3**

Lady on the bench behind me at a park in santa monica, an introduction to my love of the protection of trees.

The woman in the egg who told me "why she had to explain to me WHY SHE DID THIS",

NO DOGS ALLOWED PALLASADES BEACH SIGN

SOPHIA – EARTHS NAME.AND HER DISAPPEARANCE IN "ASTROLOGICAL READINGS", WHAT IS SHE, THIS STORY IS VERY ELUSIVE.

STARS SPLITING APART IN THE SKY – EXPLOSION IN CLEAR SKIES WHERE I CANNOT MAKE MISTAKES … THEN I HAVE TO ASK "WAS THAT A STAR?", rocks and water?

RAINBOW SEEN IN GAYLAND SO PROMINENT IN THE SUNNY DAY I WAS SHOCKED OTHERS DIDN'T NOTICE THIS.

A WAVE OF ENERGY WHICH MADE ME FEEL CHILDLIKE OVER MY LOCAL T-MOBILE STORE IN DTLA AND THIS WAS AS I WAS IN THE OHONE TRYING TO BEG FOR MY OHONE TO STAY ON.

**MY ANGELIC INITIATION**

*WHERE I SAT IN THE MIDDLE OF ALL THESE AS ONE OF BOTH ENERGIES ON BOTHE SIDES BUT MY PLACE WAS CENTER OF THEM STILL TRYINGVTO FIGURE THIS AS ITS PERSONAL AND I WANTBTO EXPLORE INTO A FILM OF ITS OWN AND THINKNITVREKATES TO MY ACCEPTENCENOF THE "EARTH ANGEL" PHEONOMINA of knowing I Am One*

**SHOE DOG**

This booknis after my strange experience which led me to develop a loving curiostity of NIKE.

Without to much at present her muse status is interesting and her relationship between her and athena is interesting, they sit in oricle cards and are used as meditations and are known to me as maybe the first of feminist in a land where my Greek plays came from.

*FINAL NOTE FOR THE PYSCHIC ATTACKERS WHO WEARS THE CLOTHES OF "AD"*
*in the aspect of humans, Prime Light has many times felt their presence amongst humans*
*to be a hindrance, the negatives of reincarnation, rebirth, all the cycles "RE" and stated the*
*Laws Of Free Will are not something earth had and cannot be taken away since it created*
*the earth and therefore in the cycle of humans coming through that aspect of life will not*
*be YHEIR as nature will NATRUALLY dictate to you how to live AND YOU WILL DO IT!*

TWO UNIQUE MENTORS OF MIND CONTROL METHODS IN THE REVERES a women
Caroline MYSS and DARIOUS MEIBODI.

## DYSLEXIC Vs THE AD+ MOVEMENT

THIS IS A CULTURE AND MOVEMENT THAT DOES NOT NEED TO BE EXPLAINED IN MY BOOK
AS MANY BOOKSTORES HAVE DEDICATED ALMOST YJE WHOLE LEARNING SECTIIN TO THIS
CULTURE OF PEOPLE IN EDUCATION WHO GROW INTO THE WORKPLACE.

LIKE MYSELF A DYSLEXIC, IT SEEMS YOU ARE NOTHING AROUND THEM IF YOU SAY YOU ARE
DYSLEXIC, AS THE PHRASE "EVERYONE IS DYSLEXIC" IS THROWN BACK AT YOU AS A FORM
OF SELF DEFENSE.

MY STRANGE EXPERIENCE 3 IS BASED ON THIS WITHIN AND AROUND A TIME IN AMERICA
WHEN EVERYONE WAS SCREAMING "DO YOUR JOB" AND A CERTAIN SECTION OF SOCIETY
HAD, HAD ENOUGH OF THE MISERABLE OLD WHITE GUY WITH TOOO MUCH MONEY, NO
COMMIN SENSE, OVER BEARING AGGRESSION LEADING TO VOILENCE THAT "IT" COULD NOT
AND MOSTLY "WOULD" NOT JUSTIFY, ALONG WITH SOCIAL MEDIA BE USED TO HELP THISE
WHO PROTESTED WITH VARIOUS CAMPAIGNS AND MORAL ETHICS BEEN YHROWN AT PEOPLE
LIKE, LETS SAY "THE ENGLISH" WHO ARE KNOWN TO BE COMPLAINERS.

IT HAS BEEN A BIT DIFFICULT WITH THE OLD JOKE OF "YOU HAVE AN ACCENET", OR FINDING
OUT YOUR FRIEND "OF THE MOMENT" IS AN ANGLOPHILE OR EVEN YOUR WORK COLLEGUE
TO A DEGREE IT HINDERS ANY RELATIONSHIP PRESENT OR TO COME.

NON AMERICANS KNOW THIS VERY WELL, ESPECIALLY THOSE WHO LIVE AND WORK IN
AMERICA WITH AMERICANS AS SOME SEEM FORTUANATE TO PROPORTION THEMSELVES
LIKE THE 60% OF AMERICANS WHO HATE BEEN AROUND "<u>DUMB AMERICA</u>".

## INTUITION Vs PYSCHIC

The reason I put this heading is; within the last 5 years of investing my time and trust in the TAROT
CARD reading system, MB AMERICA".

MY USE OF SPRIRITUAL MENTORS WAS AND IS A "GOOD EXAMPLE" OF HOW TO KEEP "TELLING
TJEM OFF", WHEN AND IF THEY PERSIST BY EXPLAINING EDUCATIONAL BASICS OF HUMAN
FUNCTIONS – WHICH EVERYINE HAS AND YET NOT EVERYONE FOR WHATEVER "HUMAN
REASON" USES TJEM TO THE BEST OF "THE" ABILITIES TO CO-CREATE A PEACEFUL CREATION
OF EXISTENCE.

which I had from the Bohdi Tree Bookstore via Michael Wamback and his wife Krista Swimmer, not dismissing Doreen Virtue's weekly online and yearly – though Ms Virtue went through a spiritual crisis and choose to EXPLORE the Teachings of Jesus and stick to "A Michael and other angels", she is accustomed to from the volumes of various bibles known to her childhood and teach them for awhile.

LITTLE DID SHE KNOW OR EVEN WANTED TO PARTAKE IN THE MADNESS OF AMERICA WHICH SHOWED ITSELF FROM HER DECISIONS AND THEN THE EMERGENCE OF DONALD TRUMP AS THE AMEICAN PRESIDENT WHILE SOCOIETY AS A WHOLE AROUND THE WORLD GEARS UP FOR THE NEW MILLENNIUM AS WE COME TO THE CLOSE OF THE 21ST CENTURY WHICH STARTED :

## MONDAY JANUARY 1ST 2001 ENDING DECEMBER 31ST 2100

The Virtue crisis is questionable and like Shakespeare's work we are all quietly feeling and doing VARIOUS hardcore revisions in this time of what is now known as THE DARK SIDE OF AQUARIUS. For this period of time I fell into the Teachings of Caroline Myss via Robert Ohotto and Collette Baron Reid.

Going back to me and Tarot Reading, the word, meaning and use of PYSCHIC became a dirty word and was changed to INTUITIVE Psychic or Medium, in this time we are asked to accept and explore our charts properly with Ciron / Kyron and the various Lilith's throughout our charts, prepping us for other names we may not have or be accustomed to yet they are there, which made me think A LOT about SIRIUS STAR system A & B as they are supposed to be our TRUE guides and were used by all the world's cultural ancestors.

So, in hindsight what I have been trying to say to those when I say "I am DYSLEXIC" is that, it is a gift and that I am NATURALLY psychic but I've ALWAYS used the words intuitive and intuition …. This is where I will explain and hopefully you will understand why I have been calling my psychic attacks STRANGE EXPERIENCES through this TAROT READING TRANSCRIPT and from the others, those experiences should have been more like my NATRUAL PYSCHIC AWAKENING like the many of us today who go through the stage 5 process in PEACE. It is meant to be a peaceful awakening of awareness which is clear and connected to all of the individual's gifts.

*[THIS IS WHERE the collective airspace should be governed in full by the individual working in themselves and their direct connection to their HIGHER SELF AND THE CREATOR as a PRIVATE CONNECTION-The Creator like us has many names but most of society uses THE NAME "GOD"]*

## SUMMER 2014 – MICHEAL WHAMBACK TAROT TRANSCRIPT
## MYSTIC JOURNEY BOOKSTORE

"….SERVES THEM RIGHT, THEY DON'T DO WHAT THERE SUPPOSED TO DO, FIRST OF ALL, RIGHT NOW AS YOU SIT HERE, I THINK YOUR EXPECTATIONS ARE REALISTIC, A LOT OF THE THINGS YOU LOVE TO SEE HAPPEN AND A LOT OF THE THINGS YOUR HOPINGBFOR SHOULD COME. TO PASS. I THINK THAT'S A GIOD THING AND FOLLOW YOUR DREAMS IS A GOOD IDEA AND YOU SHOULDN'T SECIND GUESS ANYTHING.

ONCE YOU'VE MADE A DECISION YOU SHOULD TRUST YOU ARE MAKING THE RIGHT DECISION AND SORTA SEE THINGS THROUGH AND KEEP MOVING FORWARD AND DON'T SECOND GUESS, CLEARLY IF YOU SECOND GUESS YOU DON'T KNOW WHAT YOUR DOING AND HAVE NO IDEA

BUT I THINK YOUR JUDGEMENT IS PRETTY GOOD AND YOUR KARMA IS PRETTY GOOD AND YOU SHOULD TRUST YOUR INTUITION AS YOU'VE DEALT WITH ALL THE THINGS YOU NEED TO DO, THERE'S NOTHING REALLY HOLDING OR STOPPING YOU AND YOU DON'T HAVE ANY BAGGAGE AND I LIKE THAT YOU'VE DONE WHAT YOU NEED TO DO WITH THINGS NO MORE NO ILLESS.

YOUR NOT WASTING ANY TIME OR ENERGY OR NEGLECTING ANYTHING, YOUR INSTINCTS ARE AS GOOD AS YOUR RATIONAL MIND, SO YOU JUST RELAX AND DO YOUR THING AND BE YOURSELF AMD YOU SHOULD DO REALLY WELL, AND THE OTHER THING WHICH IS REALLY NICE IS WHEN YOUR INTUITION IS GOOD IS THAT YOUR TIMING IS WELL SO YOU SHOULD BE AT THE RIGHT PLACE AT THE RIGHT TIME".

ME (Marcia, interrupt his flow of my read with) "THIS WILL ACCOUNT FOR MY DÉJÀ VU" MICHEAL "WELL YEAH!".

THIS TRANSCRIPT IS ROUGHLY 2 MINUTES OF MY 30 MINUTE TAROT READ WITH MICHEAL, HIS READINGS HELPED PERPELL ME INTO DOINGBTHIS BOOK AMD CONTINUE AND START MY OYHER PROCESSESS OF CCREATIONS.

MICHEAL READINGS LAST ANYWHERE FEOM 3 – 10 YEARS BUT HE LIKES TO STICK TO 3, I HAD 2 DONE WITHIN THE YEAR AND BOTH STOOD AS ACCURATE TO WHERE I WAS HEADING IN MY LIFE AND KEEPING MY ENERGIES TO MY SELF IN THE WAY THAT I HAD DESIRED TO USE WITH WHAT I KNEW TO BE TRUE WITH AND FOR ME …. THEN THE FORCEFUL ELEMENT'S OF VARIOUS NEGATIVE PEOPLE STARTED TO PLAY WITH MY BELIEFS AND ALL THINGS 3.

THAT'S WHY MICHEAL COULDN'T BE BOTHERED WITH PEOPLES ENERGIES OF THAT NATURE COS HE KNEW THEY WOULD DEAL WITH THE CREATORS LAW AND BE MADE AWARE AS TI WHERE THEYVARE MEANTVTO BE AND TO STOP TESTING THISE WHO HAVE GOOD INTUITION IN THE NAME OF METATPHYSICS, REGARDLESS OF THE KEVELS OF ENERGY WITHIN THE RELMS IT MAY EXIST ….

"IT"
BEEN
"A HUMAN BEING = LIGHT BEING" Vs God aka Source, Prime, Spirit etc

**KRISTA SWIMMER TRANSCRIPT – EARLY 2020**
**MYSTIC JOURNEY BOOKSTORE**

I WAS HAVING A DISCUSION WITH HER ABOUT MY DYSLEXIA AND "SOMEONE / SOMETHING" PLAYING WITH MY DYSLEXIA

KRISTA "…JUST TO FINNISH OFFTHUS THOUGHT ABOUT INTUITION, ACCORDING TO ALICE BAILEY'S BOOK….."
ME (MARCIA) "IHIDE BEHIND THAT WORD LIKE A MUTHERFUCKER UNTIL.I KNOW WHAT'S GOING IN…"
KRISTA "WELL, NO, SERIOUSLY ACCORDING TO ALICE BAILEY'S BOOK, INTUITION IS A VERY SPECIFIC THING AND IS THE HUGHEST FORM OF PYSCHI-IS-UM BECAUSE ITS THAT OF CLAIRVOYANCE AND CLAIRAUDIENT WHICH IS IN THE LOWER ASTRAL PLANE FIELD, WHERE AS INTUITION IS THE CONNECTION WHICH GOES STARIGHT TO GOD aka SOURCE.

[AS I WROTE THAT PART OF HER TRANSCRIPT 1ST APRIL 2020 A SOUND OF A SINGLE CROW IS HEARD TO INSTIGATE THIS POINT TO BE TRUE. I HAVE HAD MANY CTOW EXPERIENCES AT THE APPROPRIATE TIMES SINCE MY DÉJÀ VU AND DYSLEXIA AND PENEAL GLAND AND CHAKRAS AND KUNDALIN GOT BLOWN AS I WAS GOING THROUGH MY "5 STAGES OF SPRIRTUAL ASCENSION" …. THE CROW ALWAYS INSTIGATED I WAS CORRECT IN MY INTUITIVE THOUGHTS FEELINGS AND ACTIONS AND CORRECT WITH MY INTINCTS AND RE-VISIONS]

**WE ARE TO TRUST :**
**SOURCE,**
**SPIRIT,**
**GOD,**
**PRIME**

…. FOR ME, IT WILL.ALWAYS BE MY PRIVATE CONNECTION AS A "WHOLE BEING = LIGHT BEING" AND MY RELATIONSHIP WHICH MEANS "ITS NOT REALLY ANYONES BUISNESS UNTIL THEY "WHO, GO OUT OF THEIR WAY TO PUT YOU OFF YOIR TRACK OF SPIRITUAL GTOWTH / PATH ARE THEN TOLD!

MY CONVERSATION WITH KRISTA WENT ONTO HOW I FLOW THROUGH MY LIFE AND SHE GAVE ME A CURRENT EXAMOLE OF NEW STUDIES "REGARDING SOME WOMEN WHO WERE DOING OR STUDYING FLOW", ITS NOW A NEW THING TO CREATE, MOVE OR LIVE IN A FLOW PROGRAM – THESE ARE NEW ADAPTIONS TO THE NEUROLINGUISTIC PROGRAMMING CULTURE, WITH THE METAPHYSICS AKA NEW AGE AND SCIENCE MERGING INTO INE EEXISTENCE. THIS IS WHAT I AM AWARE ARTIFICUAL INTELLIGENCE "AI" TO BE …

PEOPLE AUTOMATICALLY THINK ROBOTS BUT ROBOTS WERE DESIGNED FROM US FOR US AS US.

IN 2020 WE SEE A WORLD OF MORE ADHD PEOPLE'S IN THE PLANET AND CHILDREN TO COME THAN DECADES PAST AND AS A DYSLEXIC PERSON, WHICH IS A GIFT OF THE MIND AND FOR THE MIND BY SOURCE AKA GOD.

MY PERSONAL STATEMENT IS ARGUABLE AND ANYTHING I DO OR SAY TO SOMEONE FROM THE "I DON'T GIVE OR KNOW HOW OR WHAT CONSTRUCTIVE CRITICISM IS" WILL FIND AN ARGUMENT WITH MY STATEMENT ABOUT WHAT IS DEEMED A GIFT WITHIN THE AD CULTURE AND THE DYSLEXIC CULTURE. THE AD CULTURE HAS BEEN SCIENTIFICALLY PROVEN TO BE OTHER THAN NORMAL OR DYSLEXIC HUMAN AND SEEM TO BE A BIGGER PROBLEM WITH THE LEARNING INFULSTRUCTURES OF THE LEARNINGBSOCIETIES AROUND THE WORLD AND IN THE WORKPLACE … WHICH IS A LEARNING STRUCTURE OF PERSONAL GROWTH IN SOCIETY WETHER IN SPIRIT LEARNING OR NOT.

*THOUGH THE BASIS OF ALL LEARNING FROM SOURCE IS :*

*THE META LANGUAGE IS "LOVE FIRST" …..*

*AND WE HAVE RUINED THIS AS WE EXPLORE WHAT THIS "LOVE" IS*

# SCENE PITCHES FOR FILM SCRIPT

## THE COMPLEXITIES OF NIKE & ATHENA

*"A SHOWRUNNER" PITCH FOR THE SCI-FI CHANNEL"*

by Maria Battise - 2019 Draft 1

### SCENE 1.

**MESSENGER** :
THR33
THIS IS YOUR MESSAGE SENT BY THE MARCIA OF THE STONES OF MARCIA'S

**RECIPIENT** :
3

**MESSENGER** :
YES
THR33

**RECIPIENT** :
OF THE MARCIA'S OF THE STONES WHERE ARE YOU FROM

**MESSENGER** : AWAY

**RECIPIENT** : AWAY
MY ROBES HAVE A HARD TIME UNDERSTANDING AWAY

**MESSENGER** : WILL
I AM TO WAIT UNTIL YOU RESPOND

**RECIPIENT** : AND THE TEXT
IT IS NOT SHORT

**MESSENGER** :
THAT IS THE WHOLE MESSAGE

**RECIPIENT** :BUT THAT IS A VERY SHORT MESSAGE

**MESSENGER** : NO
IT IS THE WHOLE MESSAGE OF THE MARCIA'S

**RECIPIENT** : AWAY
IS WHERE YOU PEOPLE ARE FROM

**MESSENGER** :
YOU DO NOT KNOW US
IT WAS WISE FOR MARCIA TO MAKE SURE SHE IS KNOWN IN HER LANDS

**RECIPIENT** :
AM I A MARCIA OF AWAY

**MESSENGER** :
THAT IS WHY THE MARCIA'S WANT TO KNOW
WHO IS AND WHERE ARE HER MARCIA'S FROM THIS LAND AS IT IS APART OF THE LAND YOU
CALL AWAY.

**RECIPIENT** :
I DID NOT CALL YOUR LAND AWAY YOU DID

**MESSENGER** : NO
I SAID I WAS FROM AWAY

**RECIPIENT** :
DO YOU LIKE MY FRIENDS

**MESSENGER** : I SEE
WHERE

**RECIPIENT** :
MY FRIENDS ARE HERE

**MESSENGER** :
MY ROBES ARE HERE AND WILL TAKE YOUR MESSAGE AND RESPOND

**MESSENGER** :
THEN THE MARCIA IS AMONGST THE ROBES

**RECIPIENT** :
I AM CONFUSED BUT HAVE GOOD MEDICINE FOR PEOPLE OF THE LIGHT CALLED SUN STAR.

**MESSENGER** :
YOU TAKE YOUR SUN STAR AND I WILL WAIT FOR MY MESSAGE AND TAKE IT BACK TO MARCIA

**RECIPIENT** :
BEFORE YOU GO CAN YOU SHOW ME AWAY

**MESSENGER** :
YOU HAVE EARTH TO GIVE YOU EXAMPLE

**RECIPIENT** : EARTH?

**MESSENGER** : YES
EARTH
WHY ARE YOU LOOKING AWAY FROM YOUR SUN STAR

**RECIPIENT** :
MY ROBES HAVE SAID IT WILL TAKE TIME

**MESSENGER** :
I SEE NO ROBES
BUT YOUR FRIENDS ARE EVERYWHERE AS YOU SAY

**RECIPIENT** : I NEED TO

**MESSENGER** :
AH,

**MESSENGER** :
YOU KNOW THE MARCIA'S DONT YOU
ARE TESTING ME BECAUSE YOU SPOKE TO ME BY BEING AWAY

**RECIPIENT** : YES
I HAVE NOT USED THIS LANGUAGE FOR A LONG WHILE AND MY ROBES ARE IN THIS LANGUAGE
ALSO

**MESSENGER** : SEEK MY FRIENDS I WILL BE BACK
I HAVE TOLD MARCIA YOU **NOTES**
*THE SCENE IS ABOUT THE USE OF*
*MEDIUMSHIP IN TODAY'S SOCIETY PRACTICES OF THE WORLD.*

*THROUGH CONSISTENT RESEARCH OF STORIES TOLD THROUGH "MEDITATION, MYTH,*
*ARGUMENTATIVE SCIENCE, ETC" WE AS PEOPLES HAVE FOUND THESE STORIES TO HOLD*
*TRUTH AND ARE EXPLORING WHAT THIS "CONSCIOUS HUMAN BEING LOOKS LIKE OR HAS*
*BECOME.*

**THE CITY WITHIN THE CITY**
scene 2 : ATHENA – THE MESSENGER

*Female ruler of a city within a CITY has to send an open message to the one to unleash truths from all to the the*
*city within the city so the woman can walk amongst them with her s????*

**FEMALE RULER**
I want all the people to stand up
I want all the people to acknowledge
I want all the people to accept
I want all the people to know the one who knows me
I want all the people to let the one back in
I am a ONE and I let the one in me and acknowledge, accept and therefore show you an example of "A"
one who is me like the ONE.

No more confusion
*These (OPEN interrogation of a healing tool)*
They say what I have said
BUT YOU ALL …..

## THE CITY WITHIN THE CITY
scene 2

**FEMALE RULER**
"transit periods and squinted of the eye beings have problems with *THEMSELEVES* Solisty refuses to let people sleep
the people of Solisty have left themselves and keep giving me the squinting eye

*RHOBES* ive released
trust is no longer within me for them the healing has become dark
and those that heal I have also dismissed

Solisty and it's people live within my home not of my request or permission

the twins of the SACRAS have been forwarding my messages, let alone respecting what the one,

has installed within us all

*INSTINCTS*
I now am nature
my kindom was never mine
but my soul of spirit of the one is truly mine".

PASS THIS TO THE ONE I REQUEST THE ONE
IT IS TIME TO COME

You
Be careful when you say particular word

The word looks like this

*"Ku - Da"*

**ATHENA**
Ku - Da?

**FEMALE RULER**
Yes. There is an ending to the word
I don't want you to say it

**ATHENA**
who do I take with me

**FEMALE RULER**
This is why I don't want you to say the ending of the word. NOW
who do you think?

*ATHENA LEAVES WITH THE EYE SET ON THE 2 L's FOR COMPANION ALONG HER JOURNEY ...*

they are lilith and lucifer end scene

**SCENE : THE VILE CUNTS**
**THE COMPLEXITIES OF NIKE & ATHENA**

MARCIA :

YOU TWO STAND UP COME HERE AND BOW - STAY IN THAT

POSITION YOU WHY AND THE MAN WHO ARE OLDER THAN

THESE TWO LET THIS HAPPEN? IN THE SPACE CALLED VISTA

BASED HERE ON HOLLYWOOD BLVD IN MY HOME …. WHY WHY

HAVE YOU ENTERED WITHOUT MY PERMISSION

FAST FASTER FASTEST IS A

PR LINE WHERE DID YOU

AQUIRE THIS LINE

I GIVE YOU A MOMENT TO TELL ME THE TRUTH AFTER THAT THE

TWO THAT ARE BOWING THERE FEET ARE GONE COS I KNOW YOU

ARE NOT TELLING ME THE TRUTH

BY THE WAY THERE BODY SHAKES, SO HURRY UP.

REST OF YOU DONT ACKNOWLEDGE THEM WE ARE GOING

TO TALK NOW. I CALLED YOU SO YOU ALL CAN TELL ME

WHO PUT THIS IN MY HEAD.

VILE CUNT 1 –
IT HAS YOUR PRINTS IN IT

VILE CUNT 78

SPEAK AND TELL THERE NOT WANTED PERIOD.

*SPEAKERS STEP FORWARD*

READY SPEAK

**SCENE DESCRIPTION** :

ALL THE SPEAKERS START TO SPEAK AS THE WATCHES WITH EYES GLARING AT THE BOWERS

*NOTE*

*OTHER ELEMENTS OF THE SCENE - FROM THE LEFT RE CAMERAS ALL THESE EYES DROP OUT OF SOMEONES HEAD*

## POEM 1 - I'M 25

I APPRECIATE MARCIA YOUR CARING,
BUT
I'M 25

EVERYTHING GOES THROUGH ME
I'M 25

YOUR MEANT TO DO WHAT I SAY
I'M 25

WHY AREN'T YOU SMOKING POT ANYMORE
I'M 25

STOP ASKING ME.QUESTIONS
I'M 25

HOW DARE YOU NOT LEAVE FROM MY SHITTY EVICTION NOTICE
I'M 25 …. I GAVE IT TO YOU OVER THE WEEKEND …. I'I'M 25

I WILL NOT TALK TO YOU …. YOU GOT AN ADULT TO TELL ME WHAT TO DO
I'M 25

I WILL COME HOME REALLY REALLY REALLY REALLY LATE
I'M 25

MARCIA, WE WILL TALK WHEN I AM 26
IN THE MEANTIME, PLEASE LEAVE SO I CAN STAY … 25

## POEM 2 – PSYCHO Vs COMMON SENSE

IT DOES NOT MATTER WHAT YOU DEEM AS LIGHT
YOUR LIGHT IS LIGHT

LIGHT IS LIGHT

YOUR SPIRITUAL PATH IS DIFFERENT TO MINE
THAT IS WHY IT IS CALLED A SPIRITUAL PATH

THERE IS NO RIGHT
THERE IS NO WRONG

YOUR SPIRITUAL PATH IS DIFFERENT FROM MINE

THE LIGHT THAT IS FOR YOU
IS DIVINE SELF – YOIR SELF

WE ARE HERE TO SERVE
TRUE SOURCE CREATION

YOUR SPIRITUAL PATH IS DIFFERENT TO MINE

4 GARDENS OF EDEN
THOSE ARE 4 CREATED THROUGHOUT
ALL SPACE AND TIME

YOUR JOURNEY HAS TO BE TRUE
OUR PATH DEPART
YOU GO YOUR WAY
I GO MY WAY

YOUR SPIRITUAL PATH IS DIFFERENT TO MINE

STAY OPEN TO THE WORLD
AND ALL WILL COME TO YOU
YOUR PATH IS YOUR PATH
AND MY PATH IS MY PATH

STOP STALKING ME

YOUR SPIRITUAL PATH IS DIFFERENT TO MINE

## POEM 3 –
## METRATRON MICHEAL LUCIFER LILITH

THE FOLLOWING IS AN EXPERIENCE, WHICH BY THE NATRUAL OCCURRENCE OF MY OWN
RELATIONSHIP TO THE ABOVE MENTIONED IS; POETIC.

LADY SHIKAAL SHEENA, AN INSTRUCTOR PF MEDITATION
BLACK COFFEE
SYMBOLISM FOR RACISM
HOMOPHOBIA
A MESSAGE FROM EMMANUEL
THERE ARE 7 ELEMENTS OF THE KABALIAN AND HE IS ONE : GENDER

A DARK ARTS ASSUMPTION
MY LOVE FOR GODDESS NIKE
SHE HAD A RELATIONSHIP WITH ATHENA

WOMEN – WOMEN

FEMINISM
ITS 2020
I'M FORCED TO ASSERT MY FEMALE LAW UPON A RETARDED MAN

TALES BEFORE LUMERIA
MEDITATE WITH ME
ARCH TO ARCH

INTO THE UN-KNOWN
OF THE HISTORY OF THE GREEKS
WOMEN RULED AND HAD MEN AS ….

EMMANUEL, WELL

WHERE ARE YOU
IN THE USA
WHAT DID THEY HAVE HERE AND STILL DO

OH, OH, OH,
SERVANTS, YES, WOMEN HAD MEN AS SERVANTS

A LESBIAN ACCEPTED AS GAY
ALL TRANSACTIONS ARE SAFE
WITHOUT GOING INTO UNIVERSAL DEFINITIONS

WHY MUST I JUST BE GAY

GENDER PRINCIPAL
GENDER LAW
DIVINE DIVINITY EXPLAINED

GO FUTHER THAN THE AVERAGE MINERAL
GO FURTHER THAN THE AVERAGE CRYSTAL
THAT IS USED WITHIN YOUR HOUSE

AND RE-PLAY WITH YOUR CRYSTALS
I AM IN THE TALE
ONE IS DIFFICULT
THE OTHER IS FANCIFUL

LUMERIA
MY FRIEND
LUMERIA

IN THIS DAY AND AGE
YOU WILL
HAVE
TO
RE – DO
IT
AGAIN

YOU MIGHT AS WELL
AS YOU ARE
ONE WHO KNOWS
BUT DID NOT KNOW
YOU KNEW

CRYSTALS?

SOLIDS, DUST, LIQUIDS AND OILS

THEY CAN BE USED UPON YOUR BODY
REMEMBER THE STORY OF A BABY WHO NEEDED THEM
IT IS IN A COMMON BOOK

YOU WILL KNOW AMD YOU WILL USE ALL.OF MY MEDITATIONS
I GUARD ALL THAT IS SECRET IN YOU
THE OTHERS WILL KILL THOSE WHO TRY

TO DO HARM TO YOU

REMEMBER ME ARCH
ARCH TO ARCH
WE LOVE ALL OF YOU
AND YOU ARE OUR FIRST

M

# ABOUT THE AUTHOR

AS AN ACTOR, MARCIA WOULD LIKE TO WRITE THE ABOVE FOR THE SCI-FI NETWORK AND BECOME A SHOW-RUNNER.

MARCIA IS STARTING OFF THROUGH A "METHODICAL PROCESS OF UNDERSTANDING MYTH, FOLKLORE & MEDITATION VISUALIZATIONS INTO 'ACTUAL HUMAN REALITIES' FROM THE HELP OF HER MENTORS WHO ARE THE 'ARCHITECT COMMUNITIES' AROUND THE WORLD!

THIS SITE WILL HELP HER FIND WAYS TO "MENTORS" FOR EXPLORATIVE & DIVERSE WAYS TO DEVELOP HER WRITING SKILLS, FOR ENTERTAINMENT & EDUCATIONAL PURPOSES.

IN ORDER TO HELP HER EXPLORE HER "CREATIVE WRITING" SKILLS, SHE WANTS TO PORTRAY IMAGERY FOR SCREEN LIKE POETRY WITHIN HER PROJECTS.

** THIS IS IMPORTANT AND SOMETIMES AN UNUSUAL THING TO DO, HOWEVER, THE WRITER MUST STAY IN THE SPACE OF WRITING WITHOUT FALLING INTO THE TRAPPINGS OF "WRITERS BLOCK" - WHICH SHE FINDS COME FROM THE BUSINESS ASPECT OF THIS PROFESSION AS WELL AS LIFE INTERFERENCE FROM WHAT WE CALL VAMPIRES OF LIFE ...

Education: MOUNTVIEW THEATRE SCHOOL (UK)

Memberships: SAG-AFTRA / BAFTA LA (USA)

Certifications / Awards: SIR ANTHONY HOPKINS, LILIAN BAYLIS AWARD (OLD VIC THEATRE UK), LAMDA & THE RALPH RICHARDSON MEMORIAL AWARDS

Areas of Expertise: PROFESSIONAL CLASSICAL ACTOR & SCREEN ACTOR

Printed in the United States
By Bookmasters